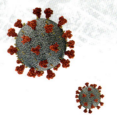

SOCIETY AND CULTURE DURING COVID-19

BY CYNTHIA KENNEDY HENZEL

CONTENT CONSULTANT
Allen Furr, PhD
Professor Emeritus of Sociology
Auburn University

Essential Library
An Imprint of Abdo Publishing
abdobooks.com

ABDOBOOKS.COM

Published by Abdo Publishing, a division of ABDO, PO Box 398166, Minneapolis, Minnesota 55439. Copyright © 2023 by Abdo Consulting Group, Inc. International copyrights reserved in all countries. No part of this book may be reproduced in any form without written permission from the publisher. Essential Library™ is a trademark and logo of Abdo Publishing.

Printed in the United States of America, North Mankato, Minnesota.
052022
092022

THIS BOOK CONTAINS RECYCLED MATERIALS

Cover Photo: Shutterstock Images
Interior Photos: Shutterstock Images, 4, 12, 26, 36, 44, 59, 70, 85, 90; Braulio Jatar/Sopa Images/Sipa USA/AP Images, 6; Everett Collection/Shutterstock Images, 11; Kyodo/AP Images, 14; Jae C. Hong/AP Images, 19; Jeffrey T. Barnes/AP Images, 21; Mark Ralston/AFP/Getty Images, 24; Fabian Ponce Garcia/Shutterstock Images, 31; Monkey Business Images/Shutterstock Images, 34; Alex Menendez/MENEA/AP Images, 40; Syda Productions/Shutterstock Images, 42; Noam Galai/Getty Images Entertainment/Getty Images, 46; Den Photos/Shutterstock Images, 50; Caitlin Ochs/Reuters/Alamy, 52; Rich Schultz/Getty Images Sports/Getty Images, 54; Ringo Chiu/Shutterstock Images, 56; Joshua Roberts/Getty Images News/Getty Images, 64; Red Line Editorial, 66, 76; Chris Zoeller/The Courier/AP Images, 75; Sven Hoppe/Picture Alliance/DPA/AP Images, 78; Mark Felix/AFP/Getty Images, 80; Ben Hasty/MediaNews Group/Reading Eagle/Getty Images, 89; Prostock Studio/Shutterstock Images, 97; John Minchillo/AP Images, 98

Editor: Marie Pearson
Designer: Becky Daum

Library of Congress Control Number: 2021951418
Publisher's Cataloging-in-Publication Data
Names: Henzel, Cynthia Kennedy, author.
Title: Society and culture during covid-19 / by Cynthia Kennedy Henzel
Description: Minneapolis, Minnesota : Abdo Publishing, 2023 | Series: Fighting covid-19 | Includes online resources and index.
Identifiers: ISBN 9781532197994 (lib. bdg.) | ISBN 9781098271640 (ebook)
Subjects: LCSH: COVID-19 (Disease)--Juvenile literature. | COVID-19 (Disease)--Social aspects--Juvenile literature. | Social isolation--Psychological aspects--Juvenile literature. | Epidemics--Social aspects--Juvenile literature. | Health--Public opinion--Juvenile literature. | Civilization, Modern--21st century--Juvenile literature. | United States--History--Juvenile literature.
Classification: DDC 614.592--dc23

CONTENTS

CHAPTER ONE
THE SHUTDOWN
4

CHAPTER TWO
FIRST CASUALTIES: THE ELDERLY
14

CHAPTER THREE
NO MORE SCHOOL
26

CHAPTER FOUR
WORKING FROM HOME
36

CHAPTER FIVE
ENTERTAINMENT
46

CHAPTER SIX
POLITICS AND DIVISION
56

CHAPTER SEVEN
THE WORKFORCE CHANGES
70

CHAPTER EIGHT
THE COVID-19 GENERATION
80

CHAPTER NINE
HOW HAVE WE CHANGED?
90

ESSENTIAL FACTS	100	INDEX	110
GLOSSARY	102	ABOUT THE AUTHOR	112
ADDITIONAL RESOURCES	104	ABOUT THE CONSULTANT	112
SOURCE NOTES	106		

CHAPTER ONE

THE SHUTDOWN

On March 22, 2020, New York City, known as the City That Never Sleeps, became quiet. The famous theaters and department stores were shuttered. Restaurants and bars were closed. The huge lighted signs in Times Square flashed on streets empty of vehicles and pedestrians. From behind apartment windows, many residents of the city marveled at the eerie stillness. An occasional siren echoed off the buildings. The Policy that Assures Uniform Safety for Everyone (PAUSE) Program, a statewide shutdown initiated by New York governor Andrew Cuomo, had begun.

Schools in the city had closed on March 16, so students were already staying at home. The new shutdown meant that all non-essential businesses had to close, although businesses deemed essential, such as grocery stores and pharmacies, could stay open. All non-essential workers had to stay home

Times Square, usually bustling with tourists, was empty as New York City entered a lockdown to stop the spread of COVID-19.

Hospital workers and medical professionals were overwhelmed with COVID-19 patients at the start of the pandemic.

unless leaving to buy essential items such as food or prescription medicines. Only essential workers such as hospital personnel, grocery store workers, police officers, firefighters, and delivery people could go to work. No one could gather in groups with people from different households.

New York had shut down because of the growing threat of the novel coronavirus, a newly discovered virus first found in Wuhan, China. This virus would come to be known as severe acute respiratory syndrome coronavirus 2 (SARS-CoV-2). COVID-19, the disease caused by the virus, was filling hospitals and morgues. Three weeks after the first case of COVID-19 had been discovered in New York City, more than 15,000 people had tested positive in the city, with one out of eight hospitalized.[1] As numbers continued to skyrocket, hospitals and morgues overflowed into makeshift facilities. There was a shortage of medical staff and supplies, especially ventilators and personal protective equipment such as masks and gloves.

In early 2020, there was no vaccine available for COVID-19, and doctors knew little about treating the new disease. Since SARS-CoV-2 spreads through the air from person to person, the US Centers for Disease Control and Prevention (CDC) recommended people isolate from one another until the disease could be brought under control. As the days went on, cities across most of the United States shut down. Single people were often left alone in isolation from others. Families coped with children who were not used to being at home all day. Some people worked from home,

NOMENCLATURE

Coronaviruses are a family of viruses that include the virus that causes the common cold. The coronavirus that causes the disease COVID-19 was first called the novel, or new, coronavirus (nCoV) because it was unknown to science. Now it is officially called SARS-CoV-2 or SARS-2. The 2 is appended because SARS-CoV-2 is related to SARS-CoV, which caused the SARS disease outbreak in 2003. In the disease name COVID-19, the 19 is taken from the year, 2019, when the first outbreak of the disease was observed.

COUNTING DEATHS

The overall death rate in the United States soared between March 5 and April 25, 2020, as COVID-19 was spreading in the country. Of the 505,059 reported deaths from all causes in the United States in this period, 87,001 were excess deaths—deaths above the number of deaths expected based on recent history. COVID-19 caused 65 percent of excess deaths. Of those deaths not directly attributed to COVID-19, many died of nonrespiratory diseases such as heart disease and diabetes. Analysts estimate that the deaths directly attributed to COVID-19 or related to COVID-19 from this period are underestimated because doctors were unfamiliar with the disease and because undiagnosed cases of COVID-19 worsen other health problems. As a result of the disease, the average life expectancy in the United States dropped from 78.8 years in 2019 to 77 in 2020.[3]

trying to deal with the distraction of childcare and other household duties, while others had idle hours to fill. Still, by the end of April, one million people had tested positive for COVID-19 in the United States, and 63,000 had died.[2]

Weeks went by. Some people were anxious or fearful. Others were bored or angry that they could not do what they wanted to do. The initial shutdown was extended, and no one really knew when it would end. Many workers in the recreation and retail industries lost their jobs as businesses remained temporarily shut down or closed permanently. People called off summer vacations and other travel plans as airlines canceled flights and hotels emptied. Families remained apart, especially those with grandparents or other family members who appeared particularly susceptible to the disease. It seemed that overnight the entire social fabric had changed.

LEARNING FROM HISTORY

Diseases have shaped cultures and societies throughout human history. The Black Death, a pandemic of the bubonic plague, killed up to one-third of the people in Europe in the 1300s.[4] This caused a shortage of labor. As a result, people in poverty were able to demand better working conditions and wages. People set up labor associations, and they created health boards to deal with disease.

CORONAVIRUSES AND ANIMALS

Some coronaviruses affect people, and others affect animals. The coronavirus that causes COVID-19 likely originated in bats. It is rare that a coronavirus that spreads from an animal to a person can then spread between people. But it does happen, as in the case of this virus. The novel coronavirus can also spread from people to animals. Known cases have been observed in cats, dogs, big cats and primates in zoos, mink on mink farms, and white-tailed deer. There is little known about the spread or how different animals are affected, but the CDC recommends that people with COVID-19 avoid close contact with animals—even their comforting furry companions.

NOT FROM SPAIN

The 1918 influenza pandemic killed approximately 50 million people worldwide, including 675,000 in the United States, between 1918 and 1920.[5] Also called the Spanish flu, it probably did not originate in Spain. It may have come from Kansas. Other theories suggest it came from France, China, or the United Kingdom. The Spanish flu's name comes from the fact that Europe and the United States were involved in World War I (1914–1918) at the time it surfaced. Most countries blocked information on the disease because they did not want the enemy to know how it affected their soldiers. Spain was neutral in the war, so it was the only major country in the affected area reporting on the disease.

In 1793, yellow fever rampaged through Philadelphia, Pennsylvania. As a result, the Founding Fathers recognized that social, economic, and political health were tied to public health. In 1798, President John Adams promoted stricter national quarantines to prevent epidemics. He also signed the Act for the Relief of Sick and Disabled Seamen to provide care for sailors. This paved the way for the creation of the organization that would eventually be named the Public Health Service. The US Public Health Service is a group of commissioned officers in the Department of Health and Human Services responsible for fighting disease and conducting research to improve public health.

Before COVID-19, the last major pandemic that affected the United States was in 1918. The 1918 influenza

Devastating disease outbreaks have struck societies throughout human history.

pandemic killed more than 50 million people worldwide.[6] It resulted in a shift in attitudes about public health. Before the pandemic, with little knowledge of the cause of disease, people assumed that the poor were disproportionately affected by disease due to inferior genetics. Scientists discovered that this was an incorrect assumption and that disease spreads easily through unsanitary living conditions. In addition, people with poor health resulting from inadequate nutrition and health care were more susceptible to disease. The pandemic caused countries to reconsider how they could stop the spread of disease by improving living conditions and health care. Russia began the first national health-care program in 1920. It was followed by many European countries.

The pandemic caused a societal shift to governments taking responsibility for their citizens' health.

LIVES CHANGE

The hundred years between the 1918 influenza pandemic and the COVID-19 pandemic brought many changes. In 2020, scientists had a greater understanding of how disease spreads, although the first line of defense of using isolation and masks to slow the spread of disease had not changed. Scientists could create vaccines to protect people. Health care was more readily available, even if not equally available. Communication was easier, although this meant it was easier for both true and false information to spread.

Many stores and businesses required face masks to be worn during the pandemic.

By September 17, 2020, 51 percent of Americans thought their lives would change in major ways once the pandemic was over. Forty-eight percent thought they would go back to normal.[7] By the end of September, COVID-19 had already killed more people in the United States than the 1918 influenza pandemic, although the 1918 pandemic had killed more as a percentage of the overall population.[8] The COVID-19 pandemic created changes in the way people go to work and school. It changed the way people interact with each other and their governments. Some changes may be short-term. However, based on how society and culture changed after other major pandemics, it seems likely that COVID-19 will bring some permanent changes in how people live and how society functions.

> "It's my hope that we can see how public health and socioeconomic disparities are widening as a result of the COVID-19 pandemic. Ideally, this will lead us to create better systems in the future."[9]
>
> —Alexandre White, assistant professor of sociology and history of medicine at Johns Hopkins University

CHAPTER TWO

FIRST CASUALTIES: THE ELDERLY

The earliest cases of COVID-19 in the United States could be traced to international travel. The first laboratory-confirmed case within the United States was on January 20 in Snohomish County, Washington. Scientists were not sure in late January how the virus spread. Additionally, the first evidence of people with no symptoms passing the virus to others was not found in Western countries until the end of January. By the end of February 2020, 47 known cases had been identified in people who had come from China or been on the *Diamond Princess* cruise ship. Another 15 people had caught the disease while overseas.[1]

    The first groups of deaths that brought awareness of how serious the virus could be were in nursing homes. On February 29, 2020, Washington reported the

An outbreak of COVID-19 on the *Diamond Princess* cruise ship forced passengers to quarantine onboard for 27 days.

15

GOVERNOR CUOMO

In New York, Governor Cuomo was accused of hiding the number of people dying of COVID-19 in care facilities. In March 2020, he had ordered that nursing homes accept residents with COVID-19 from hospitals. Many people thought this raised the number of cases in nursing homes. The nursing facilities did not report COVID-19 deaths for people who had been residents of the nursing home but died in a hospital. Investigations by federal officials determined the reported count of deaths in nursing homes was about 50 percent lower than it was in reality.[3]

country's first known outbreak in a long-term care facility in Kirkland. It said that 27 of the 108 residents had COVID-like symptoms, as did 25 of the 180 staff.[2] Staff had been reporting COVID-like symptoms since January 29.

Once the virus gained a foothold, it spread quickly through the country, especially in settings where people gathered in close quarters, such as care facilities and prisons. There was inadequate testing to do contact tracing, which is the process of figuring out everyone who has had exposure to an infected person and notifying them of their exposure so they can quarantine until they know if they are sick too. Staff from one facility often worked at multiple locations and spread disease. Nursing home residents moved in and out of hospitals with few social distancing precautions. Visitors could spread the virus into the community.

There are about 15,000 care facilities in the United States. In the first year of the COVID-19 outbreak, each facility had on average about three outbreaks.[4] There are 1.4 million residents of nursing homes, most of them elderly.[5] Some are permanent residents, while others are there for short-term rehabilitation after surgery or illness. By June 2021, 31 percent of all COVID-19 deaths had been among staff or residents of nursing homes. In just the month of December 2020, 22,000 people died in nursing homes.[6]

PRISONS

In addition to nursing homes, prisons were hit hard by the pandemic. In Kansas, half of the prisoners in the state system had been infected by December 2020.[7] In South Dakota, 60 percent had been infected. Overall, 20 percent of all prisoners in the United States had been infected, a rate four times that of the general population. Little was done to curb the infection. In May 2020, 122 prisoners from the California Institution for Men, which had one of the first outbreaks of COVID-19, were transferred to San Quentin State Prison without testing.[8] The next day, San Quentin had its first case and by midsummer had one of the largest outbreaks in the country.[9]

NOT LIKE 1918

One significant difference between the pandemic of 1918 and the COVID-19 pandemic was the demographics most affected by the diseases. In 1918, a large group of deaths occurred in people ages 20 to 40. These were people in the workforce. They were often parents. Many deaths in this age-group left a labor shortage and huge numbers of orphans.

COVID-19 was most serious for the elderly and people with compromised, or weak, immune systems. Although testing for the virus in the United States early in the pandemic was inadequate to know how many people actually had the disease, COVID-19 seemed to affect younger adults and children much less severely than older adults.

Each death from COVID-19 was a tragedy for the family, friends, and colleagues of the victim. COVID-19 was especially devastating because the disease came on quickly. People in hospitals were quarantined to try to stop the spread of the disease.

LONG-TERM IMMUNITY

Young, healthy people between 20 and 40 years old were struck hard by the influenza pandemic of 1918. One theory is that older people had retained some immunity to a similar influenza virus that had been prevalent several decades before. They had enough immunity from the old virus to give them some protection from the new one. People under 40 had not been born at the time of the previous disease spread, so they had no immunity at all to the new virus strain.

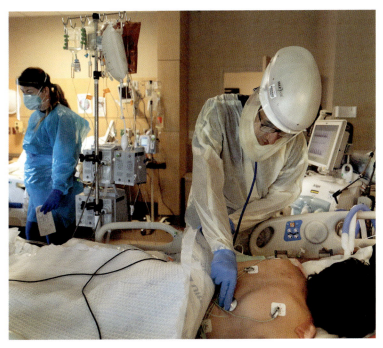

Although people older than 65 made up most COVID-19 deaths, some younger people also died of the disease.

Not even close relatives or spouses were allowed in to say goodbye to dying loved ones. The best nurses could offer was holding phones or tablets up so patients could see their families one last time on video calls.

The victims of COVID-19 were often retired. Their children were adults. Some believe that this changed how society viewed the large number of deaths. They thought that if it had been children dying at the same rates, people would have had much more concern. But because the elderly had lived long lives and were typically no longer working or raising kids, it was easier for people to not feel concerned and to find the deaths of the elderly less tragic than the deaths of young people. Some people did not recognize that many elderly people still have good lives, receiving visits from family and friends, enjoying hobbies, and participating in activities with people their own age.

STAYING HOME

Although media focused on the nursing home disaster, high rates of mortality among the elderly also created a change in how elderly people lived at home. About 93.5 percent of senior adults live at home.[10] Due to fear of COVID-19 running rampant in care facilities, fewer seniors moved to nursing homes even though they might have benefited from the services offered. Hospital admissions for elderly people outside of care for COVID-19 decreased, leaving health officials to wonder whether people were not getting the care they needed for other health issues. Nursing homes also suffered setbacks as they needed to spend more of their limited budgets on enhanced personal protective equipment, such as masks and gowns. Some had to close.

Many nursing homes did not allow visitors during the pandemic. Family members had a hard time visiting their loved ones.

Seniors who lived at home during the shutdowns did not have the same level of care from the community or from family as before. In the United States, 23 percent of the elderly living at home reported that during the shutdown they did not receive needed services such as food preparation. Nineteen percent of people older than 65 reported that they had suffered economic difficulties during the pandemic.[11] They were often isolated, unable to do the activities that kept them physically active and mentally engaged.

Then, as the pandemic continued through the summer of 2020, some young people blamed their lack of jobs and the inconvenience of lockdown on the elderly. Many of the restrictions were implemented to protect the most vulnerable—which included many people who held political power and money—while less was done to protect young adults who were less likely to get sick and more likely to have been facing economic challenges even before the pandemic. Some young people began to feel resentment and refused to stay at home or follow social distancing guidelines. As one young woman stated, "My risk tolerance is high and I refuse to stop enjoying life."[12]

Psychologists worried that the messages and restrictions that helped protect the elderly would simultaneously reinforce stereotypes about them. On one hand, seeing seniors as frail—when many are strong and healthy—could lead younger people to offer unwanted help. On the other hand, it could lead people to think that seniors are not as deserving of medical care, and possibly to apply that belief to themselves when they grow old.

AMERICAN INDIAN ELDERS

The COVID-19 pandemic took a toll on American Indian people in the United States, killing Indigenous people at twice the rate of white people. For many nations, it was a cultural crisis. The elderly have a vast understanding of the languages, stories, songs, traditions, and histories of their nations. They are respected members of their communities. "It's like we're having a cultural book burning," said Jason Salsman, from the Muscogee (Creek) Nation in eastern Oklahoma.[13]

In the vast Navajo Reservation, which covers land in Arizona, New Mexico, and Utah, many people live in remote trailers without running water. With the lockdown, community centers were closed, stranding people from getting any help. Many others lived in multigenerational families where social distancing was difficult.

> "It takes your breath away. The amount of knowledge they held, and connection to our past."[14]
>
> —Ira Taken Alive, of the Standing Rock Sioux Tribe, North Dakota, whose family lost many elders to the pandemic

A nurse checks the temperature of a Diné woman. At the start of the COVID-19 pandemic, the Navajo Nation had one of the highest infection rates in the United States.

Nations worked to protect their elders. Diné (Navajo) women began a campaign, Defend Our Community, to bring food and sanitizer to people in need. They checked on the elderly to see if they needed help. The White Mountain Apache Tribe in Arizona sent thermometers and pulse oximeters, devices to measure oxygen in the blood, to young people so they could check on their grandparents.

In some cases, nations protected their people from those outside the reservations. When South Dakota governor Kristi Noem did not mandate state restrictions to slow the spread of COVID-19, some American Indian peoples took action. In May 2020, the Oglala Sioux and Cheyenne River Sioux Tribes set up checkpoints on highways passing through their lands to keep people from spreading the disease onto their reservations. Governor Noem tried to make the Cheyenne River Sioux Tribe take down the checkpoints. The tribe refused, and the case ended up in federal court. The tribe won the case, and the checkpoints remained in place until March 2021, when the tribal council determined that the number of cases was declining.

CHAPTER THREE

NO MORE SCHOOL

On March 5, 2020, the Northshore School District in Washington became the first district to close because of COVID-19. The district, which is outside of Seattle, had already closed several schools as parents and students worried about the spread of COVID-19 from nursing homes nearby. As the death toll from COVID-19 rose, every school district in the country was closed by the end of the month.

Suddenly, 50 million public school children were at home.[1] Parents had to find childcare or quit their jobs to stay home with their children. Schools were tasked with creating platforms for online learning and providing laptops or tablets for students. Teachers learned to use new software and created online lessons practically overnight. As with other shutdowns, the first school closures were scheduled to last for a few weeks. They eventually expanded to a full month. Finally, most

During the pandemic, many students had to attend school virtually.

> ### LASTING EFFECTS
> Most children have mild symptoms and recover from COVID-19. But some children may have multisystem inflammatory syndrome after they have had COVID-19. This means that organs and tissues such as the heart, lungs, kidneys, brain, skin, eyes, and digestive system can become inflamed. It is not fully understood what causes the problem, but most children recover with medical care. The best way to avoid the syndrome is to avoid getting COVID-19.

schools simply went online for the rest of the school year.

By May 2020, 29 percent of parents thought their children were experiencing mental and emotional harm because of social distancing and school closings. But for most families, this was just the beginning. There were few activities during the summer for students. Camps closed. Sports shut down. There were no movie theaters or in-person activities with friends. In some places, public parks roped off playground equipment and removed basketball hoops.

ONLINE ONLY

As the 2020–2021 school year neared, families waited to hear whether their schools would open for in-class learning. Most did not. Schools opened online, with students signing in to class through video apps such as Zoom. Extracurricular activities such as music, sports, theater, or other special interests most often fell by the wayside.

    Online school did not work for many students because they could not get online. The National Education Association found that approximately 25 percent of households with school-age children either did not have access to the internet or did not own a device to access the internet.[2] Even those with access might have multiple students and adults sharing the same device. Sometimes, students might get on the class video call using their phone, but they could not access and complete written lessons on the phone.

    Even for students who could fully use online learning, the isolation of studying from home took its toll. Taking away the social aspects of school, an important part of the school learning experience, left many students disengaged with learning. Older students were often left with no supervision during the day while their parents worked. Many found it difficult to stay on task. Other students were responsible for watching younger siblings during the day. In many households, students had limited access to extra help with lessons, and they struggled to digest material on their own.

For many teachers, the switch to online learning was a scary and overwhelming experience. A few teachers excelled, developing innovative new models of instruction. Others struggled to adapt their normal classroom routine to an online class. As the year went on, hybrid models, where students went to school part of the time and learned online part of the time, caused more confusion. In many cases, teachers were wearing masks while instructing in-class learners and also trying to keep the attention of those watching on Zoom.

A LOST YEAR

As the year went on, schools gradually began to open. Most schools had mandates for faculty, students, and staff to wear masks and try to social distance. It was difficult to meet guidelines of social distancing to keep students safe. Crowded classrooms did not allow students to keep six feet (1.8 m) apart. There was not enough staff to clean.

The cost of the disruption in education was severe. Even a short time out of school or away from structured learning can make a difference. A study of short-term school closings for snow showed that five days of missing school caused a 3 percent drop in the passing rate for young students.[3]

Testing at the end of the disrupted 2020–2021 school year showed students on average were 3 to 6 percent behind in reading and 8 to 12 percent behind in math compared with the previous year. This translated into students in grades one through six being five months behind in math and four months behind in reading. The time out of school further widened the gap between students from wealthy and poor families, as well as the gap between white students and Black

A COVID-19 vaccine was not approved for teenagers until late August 2021. School workers checked students for symptoms to reduce the risk of spreading the virus.

and Latino students. Black and Latino students lost six months of math. White students lost four months.[4] For some students who required more personal help, like the five million English language learners and the seven million students with disabilities in the country, the loss was even greater.[5]

Of great concern to educators were students who seemed to have disappeared from the school system. These were students who did not return to classes when schools opened and had no records of transfers to other schools. The numbers were large: 12,000 missing in Dallas, Texas; 4,000 in Nashville, Tennessee; 88,000 in Florida. A small number, 3 to 5 percent, may have moved to private schools or switched to homeschooling. Many others had dropped out of school as families lost their homes or

> "What this shift [in reopening schools] has demonstrated to us is the inequities that educators have always known existed in the public education system have now been highlighted to policymakers and to the public. So I see 2021 as the pivotal year we start to address these inequities."[6]
>
> —Maureen Stover, a teacher in North Carolina

moved in with relatives. Miami-Dade County in Florida identified 10,000 missing students. By going door to door and tracking down students, officials managed to get 7,700 back into school.[7]

LOSS OF SECURITY

School for many students is more than a place to learn and socialize. Schools provide food security under the National School Lunch Program. In 2019, schools provided free or reduced-cost lunches to 29.6 million children. That number was reduced in 2020 to 22.6 million due to disruptions caused by school closings.[8] The program worked during the summer to provide money for families to feed their children and opened the free lunch

SPECIAL EDUCATION

Children who relied on special education services were among the students hardest hit by COVID-19. Often these students do best with very consistent structure, and when that structure collapsed as the pandemic hit, their parents needed to try to develop new routines to help them be successful. At the same time, when students using special education services had to do remote learning, it made it difficult for school systems. Schools, which were already overwhelmed with trying to quickly convert to an online class format, had difficulty keeping track of them and making sure they were achieving their goals.

The pandemic caused a lot of stress for students and adults. Feelings of depression and anxiety increased in the United States.

program to all students for the 2021–2022 school year. In addition to food, schools offered shelter for children without adequate housing.

Schools provide counselors for students with mental health issues or who need help transitioning from high school to college. In the United States, 13 percent of young people get mental health care from schools.[9] Counselors were overwhelmed during the pandemic, many with students dealing with changes since returning to in-person school.

Schools also provide a secure place for students who live with abusive adults. Teachers and school health-care professionals are often the first people to report child abuse. A study in Florida showed a 27 percent drop in alleged child abuse cases in March and April 2020 after schools had shut down.[10] It is unlikely that abuse stopped as families faced job losses and isolation. Abuse was simply not reported.

By the end of 2021, students had lived through at least parts of three school years with COVID-19 disruptions. Students younger than third grade had never known a normal school year. When COVID-19 vaccinations for children ages five and up were approved in November 2021, there was hope that schools could return to normal. But it would take years and a lot of help for students to catch up on what they had missed. As schools reopened, teachers had to spend time socializing students back into a school setting where they were expected to stay in their seats and pay attention to the teacher rather than play on their phones or bother other students.

CHILDREN GET VACCINATED

Although adults in the United States could get vaccinated for COVID-19 as early as December 2020, it took longer for the Food and Drug Administration (FDA) to approve the vaccination for children. Children older than 16 were approved to get the vaccines in April 2021, and those older than 12 got approval in May 2021. The FDA approved vaccines for children ages five to 11 on October 29, 2021. Vaccines for children under five were expected to be approved by early 2022.

CHAPTER FOUR

WORKING FROM HOME

As schools closed, some families embraced the time together, especially those who did not have financial stress. They took the opportunity to bond more as a family by enjoying activities, playing games, and watching movies. But there were factors beyond children studying online at home that also disrupted families. For most families, the COVID-19 shutdowns caused stress. By the end of April 2020, 30 million people had filed for unemployment. That was one in five people in the workforce.[1] This put financial stress on families. When the lockdowns closed their businesses, many adults had to stay at home.

Those who could work from home had different challenges. They needed work spaces at home. This might mean a spot in the basement or in a closet or on the kitchen table. Children doing online schooling also needed home work spaces. Families rearranged their

Many parents had to juggle the responsibilities of working full time and providing full-time childcare.

THE PET BOOM

With more people staying at home in 2020, many households decided it was time to get a new pet. Approximately 12.6 million people brought home a new animal companion.[4] Puppy sales rose by 40 percent. People adopted two million cats from places such as rescues and shelters.[5] Pets became work companions and playmates for children. Walking the dog was a good excuse to go outside. Along with the new pets, the pet supply business boomed. Veterinary businesses grew too, although like human hospital workers, they suffered from lack of space and staff. One animal hospital booked about half a million more visits in 2020 than the year before. In addition, its telehealth business doubled.[6]

houses to accommodate everyone as well as possible.

Many of those working from home learned to function with video chat meetings. These online meetings could be a challenge with children and pets roaming through the background or with intermittent internet service. Focus on work was one of the biggest issues. Some 32 percent of people reported problems getting work done due to lack of motivation or interruptions.[2] This was especially true for younger workers. Of those ages 18 to 29, 53 percent had problems with motivation to get their work done.[3] People with children also faced challenges. About 50 percent of workers who had children under 18 found it hard to work without interruption compared with 20 percent of those who did not have children.[7]

TELEWORKING

There was a sharp economic divide between those who had the option of working from home and those who did not. For workers with a bachelor's degree or greater, 62 percent could work from home. Only 23 percent of workers without a four-year degree had the option of working from home. Low-income workers were less satisfied with protection from the virus in the workplace and more likely to worry about being exposed to COVID-19 at work. Among those who went to work, 48 percent of white workers were concerned about exposure to the virus while 70 percent of Black and 67 percent of Hispanic workers were concerned.[8]

For those who had jobs that could be done from home, 20 percent were already working at home all or most of the time before the pandemic and 71 percent began working from home once shutdowns happened. By the end of 2020, many people had adjusted to working from home, with 54 percent wanting to continue to work at home at least part of the time even after the outbreak was under control.[9]

One of the most commonly mentioned advantages to working at home included more flexibility to choose work hours. By the middle of 2021, a survey showed that 61 percent of parents working at home wanted to continue at-home work full time, and 37 percent wanted a hybrid work model with working at home part time and going into a workplace part time. Only 2 percent opted for

Grocery store employees were essential workers during the pandemic. They risked exposure to the virus at work.

going back to the office full time.[10] More women than men would opt for working all of the time at home.

FAMILIES STRUGGLE

Families forced into isolation struggled with more than just space constraints. Many lost friends and family to COVID-19, and they could not mourn in the usual way with no funerals or loved ones to give in-person comfort. Other families faced illness or fear of catching the disease. They struggled to protect vulnerable family members. Childcare became a major point of stress. Not only were schools and childcare facilities closed, but social distancing kept many people from relying on friends and family for childcare.

Some families fractured under the stress. Divorces increased 34 percent from March through June 2020

THE CARES ACT

In late March 2020, the government took steps to help struggling citizens and businesses. The Coronavirus Aid, Relief, and Economic Security (CARES) Act provided money to individuals, schools, businesses, state and local governments, and public health. The largest amount of the $2 trillion bill was sent to individuals to help people pay their bills. Big corporations got a quarter of the money, while $377 billion in funds went to small businesses.[11] Small businesses had to apply for the funds, and many got nothing because the money ran out before they could apply.

Lockdowns forced couples to spend more time together, which sometimes put stress on their relationships.

compared with the same months in 2019. About one-third of couples said the reason for separation was due to the lockdown.[12] Young couples were the most likely to divorce.

Many people began to question their priorities in life. If asked, most people would say one of their top priorities is family. However, their stated priority was often not reflected in how they spent their time and energy before the lockdown. Many people spent more time at work than with family. Being forced to stay at home made some people realize they were not putting their time and energy into important things like family. As a result, some tried to spend less time working in order to prioritize family.

WOMEN ARE HARDEST HIT

Women were particularly hard-hit during the pandemic. Even before the spread of COVID-19, family caregiving was primarily the responsibility of women. At least one in ten women was caring for an adult family member, such as an elderly relative or a family member with a disability.[13] This rate rose after the pandemic began as women cared for family members affected by the disease. This was particularly true of low-income women and women of color.

One in ten women quit their jobs during the pandemic. Many quit because of fear of catching the virus or bringing it home to their families. Low-income women were three times more likely to quit their jobs than higher-income women.

> "If we can use this pandemic as an opportunity to take stock of our lives and to recommit to building the kind of people-centered life, then I think there are good things in store for us."[14]
>
> —*Vivek Murthy, surgeon general of the United States*

Black and Hispanic women, who often worked at low-income jobs, were more likely to quit their jobs than white women. Because they could not get childcare, single mothers were twice as likely to quit as women with partners.[15]

For parents, school shutdowns were a primary reason for leaving work. Three of ten women had to take time off work because of school or day care closures. For slightly less than half of mothers, this meant going without pay because their jobs did not provide paid sick leave. That increased to 65 percent for low-income mothers and 70 percent for those who worked part time. In March

Making time for hobbies helped people cope with the stresses of the pandemic.

2020, 54 percent of mothers reported that worry or stress related to COVID-19 had affected their mental health compared with 35 percent of fathers.[16]

Overall, depression in adults rose from 8.5 percent before the pandemic to 27.8 percent in the first months after the pandemic began.[17] As time went on, the problem got worse. By October 2021, the number of adults with depression rose to 32.8 percent.[18] Loneliness was another problem. Loneliness can reduce life expectancy and limit creativity. It can contribute to heart disease, dementia, depression, anxiety, and sleep problems.

FIGHTING LONELINESS

US surgeon general Vivek Murthy wrote a book called *Together: The Healing Power of Human Connection in a Sometimes Lonely World*. Published in early 2020, it was written before COVID-19. In the book, Murthy gave recommendations for dealing with loneliness. He said people should spend 15 minutes a day with those they care about by phone or letter. People should give full attention to those they are spending time with instead of being on the internet. People should serve their communities by checking on a neighbor. And people should embrace solitude by going outside or listening to music. Reviewers Carol P. Motley and Charlotte C. Linder noted that the book was very relevant to the pandemic. They said, "Today, with social isolation and recommendations that we remain at home as much as possible, we are experiencing a surge in the loneliness epidemic Murthy brings to light."[19]

CHAPTER FIVE

ENTERTAINMENT

With the shutdown of restaurants, bars, theaters, sporting events, and public gatherings, people began looking for things to do. People had hours to fill. Although most libraries closed during the shutdown, people turned to books as a way to pass the time and escape the anxiety of the real world. Sales of physical books rose 8.2 percent, with the leading genre being juvenile fiction.[1] Sales of e-books and downloads of audiobooks also rose. Some popular nonfiction books were about pandemics and self-help.

Traditional forms of entertainment surged during the months of the shutdown. Jigsaw puzzle sales went up by 300 to 400 percent, the fastest increase since the Great Depression of the 1930s. Historian Anne Williams explained her theory as to why puzzles became popular. She said, "It's something you can control. . . . It's also a challenge over which you can prevail."[2]

Theaters around the country temporarily shut down during the pandemic.

PLAGUE STORY

"The Masque of the Red Death," published in 1842 by Edgar Allan Poe, is probably the most famous plague story. The main character, Prince Prospero, isolates himself and his privileged guests in his castle, where they party in safety while a gruesome fictional disease devastates the poor throughout his realm. As the wealthy left the cities during the COVID-19 pandemic, many people remarked that they were reminded of the story—and of how people made arguments about the number of lives it was worth losing to keep the economy strong, or the party going. Poe's cautionary tale, however, ends with the Red Death slipping into the party, illustrating that even the rich cannot really isolate themselves in the long run.

Another traditional activity, board games, thrived during the shutdown. Board games are usually social. They require people to interact. Like other forms of entertainment, board games helped people move beyond reality and gave them something else to think about. By December 2020, toy and game company Mattel had seen an increase of board game sales of 48 percent.[3] People played the games within their own households. They also used video chat apps and online versions of board games to play with people outside of their homes.

SCREEN TIME

With time to fill, people turned to binge watching streamed shows on Netflix, Disney+, or other streaming services. Some shows became pandemic hits as people used social media to discuss characters and plotlines and recommend shows. Other people turned to movies, watching new films or rewatching old franchises. For the travel starved, documentaries helped people see new places.

Social media created its own form of entertainment. Performers such as John Legend, Garth Brooks, and Katharine McPhee produced online concerts as live venues were shut down due to the pandemic. Data by United Talent Agency showed that three-quarters of people surveyed attended some type of online event such as a music concert or comedy show during the pandemic. Almost nine in ten indicated that they would attend online events in the future, even if live events returned.[4] This may well be a permanent shift in

CORONA: THE GAME

The four Schwaderlapp sisters in Germany used their time during the first COVID-19 shutdown to invent a new board game based on events in the pandemic. The object of the game is to fill a shopping list for a neighbor in need. Obstacles include hoarders buying up all of the product you need, such as toilet paper, or being exposed to the virus and ending up in quarantine. Players can decide to go their own way or cooperate. The winner is the first to fill the list. The girls' father hired an artist to design the components of the game, and several thousand games had sold by Christmas 2020.

Early on in the pandemic, streaming services like Netflix saw a rise in viewership as more people were staying at home.

the way people enjoy these events. Although live events have the attraction of having a close connection with the talent and other fans, streamed events can also offer some interaction through social media and the ability to submit song requests.

Social media offered other distractions, such as TikTok dance challenges. Ohio teen Keara Wilson put her dance to Megan Thee Stallion's "Savage" on TikTok and challenged others to try her moves. Within days her dance had gone viral. With the production of new shows delayed, celebrities got together on Zoom to do reunion shows. John Krasinski, from *The Office*, started an online talk show with guests such as Brad Pitt, George Clooney, and Oprah Winfrey, helping present upbeat stories.

ENTERTAINMENT LOSERS

Not all entertainment thrived in the pandemic. Live theater struggled greatly. All 41 theaters on Broadway in New York City closed on March 12, 2020.[5] Only the ghost light, a single bulb, glowed from the stage of the dark venues. In this theater tradition, the light remains lit to keep the spirits of past actors and their characters from running amok. It was more than a year before the first theater on Broadway to reopen, the St. James, held a performance on April 3, 2021.

> "The TV is on. Or the computer is on, or some other screen is on. But something is on because everything non-screen-based is on pause."[6]
>
> —*Bill Carter, CNN, on the lockdown in April 2020*

The film industry was similarly devastated, and many in the industry predicted that the changes forced on movie companies during the pandemic would be permanent. In 2021, Warner Bros announced that on the theater release dates for all of its movies that year, the

Audience members eagerly waited for the start of the first Broadway performance since the COVID-19 pandemic began.

films would be released simultaneously on streaming services. Jonathan Kuntz, a film historian at the School of Theater, Film, and Television at the University of California, Los Angeles, predicted that the traditional model of companies sending films to movie theaters would become obsolete. People will stream movies at home rather than sit in crowded theaters.

How movies are made will change too. Production costs grew during the pandemic because of increased health and safety measures and shorter work hours. These added costs will likely remain. Already, production companies had moved to creating backgrounds digitally instead of constructing elaborate sets. Even as actors return, having huge expensive sets created by craftspeople is likely a thing of the past. It is not practical when computers can be used to create the background imagery and special effects.

SPORTS

Almost every sport, from school teams to professional leagues, shut down in the spring of 2020. Even as teams began to play, with players isolated from fans and family to protect them, stadiums remained empty. For some sports, such as golf, having no spectators was less dramatic than for sports such as hockey, where fans were a major part of the fun. Broadcasters played fan noise and put carboard cutout fans in the stands to make the TV viewing experience seem less strange. But only 22 percent of fans felt that watching live sports on TV would be much less enjoyable without fans attending.[7]

   When fans returned, some things had changed. Strict COVID-19 testing was enforced, and players who tested positive could not play. There was no high-fiving with fans or locker rooms crowded with reporters. For fans attending games, there were some perks. Although the situation may change in the future, ticket prices were generally lower, and there was greater leniency for refunds and exchanges. A more permanent change will likely be the industry's move to cash-free and paper-free ticketing.

The Phillie Phanatic, mascot for the Philadelphia Phillies, celebrates in the stands with cardboard cutouts of fans during an MLB game in 2020.

Professional sports have had to rethink the way fans interact with their favorite teams or sports stars. The shutdown has hastened the move from network and cable television subscriptions to streaming services. The streaming service Peacock, for example, has made large investments in acquiring rights to sporting events since the pandemic began.

THE OLYMPICS IN JAPAN

After many weeks of indecision, the International Olympic Committee and Japan postponed the 2020 Summer Olympic Games that were to be held in Japan. The decision was made after calls from many countries to postpone the games because of safety and health precautions. The Olympic Games had only been canceled three times in history. The 1916 Games were canceled because of World War I. The 1940 and 1944 Summer and Winter Games were canceled because of World War II (1939–1945). Japan was able to hold the 2020 Games in 2021, although there were strict COVID-19 precautions. No overseas spectators were allowed, not even family of the athletes. Athletes were tested daily. Members of the media and officials were asked to eat takeout food and dine alone instead of eating inside restaurants.

CHAPTER SIX

POLITICS AND DIVISION

Often a crisis causes people to come together to fight a common enemy and help their neighbors. Before the pandemic, the country was deeply divided between far-right conservatives and far-left liberals. President Donald Trump had been impeached by the Democrat-controlled House of Representatives but acquitted by the Republican-controlled Senate.

In a Pew Research study on the effects of the pandemic, most people felt the differences between groups in the United States were as stark as ever. One of the first big divides was political. In the study, 26 percent of respondents reported negative effects on society, politics, and safety precautions.[1] Almost no one mentioned the pandemic resulting in positive effects in these areas.

Closing businesses and schools created party-line splits. There were many consequences that politicians

Government policies required people to wear masks in airports and on flights throughout the pandemic.

had to consider when mandating shutdowns, and the consequences they prioritized tended to depend on political party. Republicans tended to focus on long-term economic and social consequences of shutdowns, from the risks of causing joblessness and long-term government dependence to mental health and public safety issues. Democrats tended to focus especially on the loss of human life issue. Issues on both sides were serious and needed to be carefully considered. The divides led to arguments that shook people's faith in the government as well as in their fellow Americans.

DISPUTES OVER MASKS

Wearing masks to slow the spread of the virus was one topic that illustrated divides in the nation. People have worn masks to try to protect themselves from disease throughout history. During the Black Death, plague doctors wore masks that looked like long beaks filled with perfume to protect themselves from what they thought was bad air causing disease. In reality, these masks did nothing to prevent the plague. During the 1918 pandemic, people wore masks. However, the masks were often made

A mask helps prevent particles of SARS-CoV-2 from spreading to other people.

of materials that were not effective in preventing viral spread, not well-fitted, and not kept clean.

Leading up to the COVID-19 pandemic, surgeons and other doctors wore surgical masks to avoid spreading diseases and infection to vulnerable patients, but these masks were not designed to prevent the wearer from breathing in virus particles. Doctors told people with compromised immune systems to wear masks, such as N95 masks, in public. N95 masks prevent people from breathing in virus particles. But asking or mandating that everyone wear masks in public to slow the spread of COVID-19 was one topic that illustrated how divided the country was. During the first months of the COVID-19 pandemic, lack of information on the usefulness of wearing masks left people in a state of confusion. As the CDC first began providing information, it did not recommend masking because there was no data at that time on exactly how the SARS-CoV-2 virus spread. However, by April 2020, once research showed an airborne spread, the CDC recommended masking. It did not specifically recommend N95s for the public because there was a shortage of masks for health-care professionals and the government wanted to make sure they did not run out. There was no consensus on whether cloth or paper masks were effective.

MAKE YOUR OWN

The United States faced a severe shortage of masks in the early months of the pandemic. As governments tried to provide what was available to health workers, first responders, and other essential workers, people began making their own masks. Instructions appeared on the internet, and homemade masks were seen everywhere. The CDC recommended using multiple layers of tightly woven cotton that would fit snugly to the face and that was machine washable. Many home crafters stepped up to make masks for friends as well as for essential workers.

They were generally too loose fitting and made of materials with a weave that did not protect the wearer from infection. There was evidence, however, that they kept the wearer from spreading the infection to others.

In April 2020, President Trump said of wearing a mask, "I don't think I'm going to be doing it."[2] Later, he did begin wearing a mask and spoke in favor of it. Some of the president's supporters followed his initial lead. As the buildup to the November elections came closer, Republicans tended not to wear masks. Democrats typically did. Those in favor of masks were more likely to see wearing a mask as part of the social contract to protect the community. Those against requiring masks often viewed mask mandates as either not a proven strategy against the virus or an overreach of government on their freedom to make their own choices.

Meanwhile, governors, especially Democratic governors, began mandating wearing masks in public

> "Masks work, but they are not infallible. And, therefore, keep your distance."[3]
>
> —*Paul Digard, virologist, University of Edinburgh, United Kingdom*

within their states. People who did not support wearing masks brought lawsuits to protect their personal freedom to make their own health decisions. Some Republican governors, including Governor Brian Kemp of Georgia, did not let cities or other communities in their states have their own mask mandates. Many counties, like Miami-Dade in Florida, mandated wearing masks anyway, setting off court battles and further dividing the government.

MASKS SAVE LIVES

One study released in June 2020 looked at states that mandated wearing masks. In April and May 2020, researchers estimated that these states had a lower rate of COVID-19 than they would have had by using only other measures like social distancing. They estimated that the rate was reduced by up to 2 percent per day. At that rate, the mandates may have prevented up to 450,000 cases.[4]

THE VACCINES

As the vaccines became available to the public, some questioned their safety and necessity. President Trump encouraged pharmaceutical companies to create a vaccine for SARS-CoV-2 as quickly as possible. Vaccines were produced in record time. By December 15, 2020, the first people were receiving their first dose. Most doctors and public health officials thought it would be a game changer. All the country had to do was get everyone vaccinated, and the problem of COVID-19 was over.

President Trump lost the election in November 2020, and President Joe Biden took office in January 2021. This meant Biden's administration would be in charge of making sure that the vaccines were distributed. The distribution began slowly as there were not enough vaccines for everyone who wanted one. Gradually, the process got better, and by day 92 of Biden's administration, 200 million shots had been administered.[5]

Once the production and distribution of the vaccines were under control, Biden faced another problem. Many people refused to take the vaccines, while others were hesitant to be vaccinated and put off getting the shot. Some did not have confidence that the government knew what it was doing, or they were suspicious that the vaccines had not been tested enough. Others did not believe COVID-19 was really dangerous, or they thought that they had natural immunity after having had the disease. Some simply struggled to get to a vaccination site. By April 2020, the number of shots given daily began decreasing. The country fell just short of Biden's goal of

Biden received his COVID-19 vaccine on television to encourage Americans to get vaccinated.

getting 70 percent of adults at least one vaccine shot by July 4, 2021.[6] Instead, 67 percent had at least one shot by that date.[7]

President Biden began using the power of his office to try to increase the vaccination rate. In September 2021, he mandated that all federal employees be vaccinated. In addition, all nursing homes and hospitals that accepted federal Medicare or Medicaid funding were to have their workers vaccinated, as were all companies with more than 100 employees.[8] The US Supreme Court later overturned the mandate for companies. Many states made their own mandates for state employees, including police and utility workers, to get vaccinated. By November 1, 2021, 70 percent of adults were fully vaccinated, and 80 percent had received at least one shot.[9]

However, forcing people to be vaccinated also created outrage. Protests were seen from Los Angeles, California, to New York City. Governors in Republican-controlled states worked with state legislatures to work around the mandates. Michelle Mello, a professor at Stanford University, identified two major groups opposing the mandates: those who opposed mandates for religious or personal reasons and politicians who wanted the support of right-wing voters. By December 2021, more than 91 percent of Democrats had had at least one dose of a vaccine, while just 60 percent of Republicans had.[10]

In the end, the pandemic left most people feeling the country was more divided than before the virus hit. In some countries, such as Denmark, people felt that the pandemic had made their country more unified, with 72 percent of people in Denmark agreeing that it had. In the United States, only 18 percent thought the country had become more unified after the pandemic struck.[11]

ETHNIC AND SOCIOECONOMIC DIVIDES

Inequity between the rich and poor in jobs, education, and financial stress were brought into sharp focus as the country shut down. People in low-wage jobs were

COVID-19 BY THE NUMBERS

VACCINATION RATES

As the divide grew between those who were vaccinated and those who were not, President Biden called the rise in COVID-19 cases and deaths during the fall of 2021 a "pandemic of the unvaccinated."[12] This was because the majority of people hospitalized with COVID-19 had not been vaccinated.[13] The Omicron variant of the virus was more efficient at spreading than previous variants, but early research indicated that it caused milder symptoms than the Delta variant. The vaccines were less efficient at preventing infection by the Omicron variant, but those who were vaccinated and still got COVID-19, or breakthrough cases, had milder symptoms. Rates of vaccination corresponded with new COVID-19 cases and deaths.[14] More Republican-led states like in the Southeast and Upper Midwest had the lowest rates of vaccination and the highest rates of hospitalizations per population. The Northeast and West Coast had the highest rates of vaccination by population.[15] However, cases rose in all areas in early 2022 due to how contagious the Omicron variant was.[16]

PERCENT OF FULLY VACCINATED PEOPLE IN EARLY FEBRUARY, 2022[17]

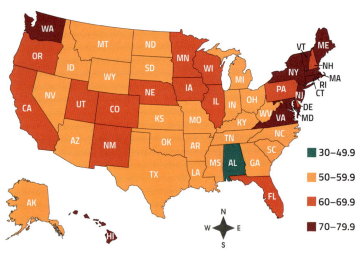

often the hardest-hit during the pandemic. They were more likely to become unemployed or work on the front lines. Workers in low-wage jobs in fields such as retail, restaurants, travel, and entertainment were among the first laid off and the last to come back. People in these low-wage jobs often had little savings to help carry them through the shutdown.

In addition, people who work low-wage jobs were more likely to work essential jobs, such as grocery store clerks and housekeepers at hospitals. These people had to keep working during the pandemic in places where they were at a higher risk of being exposed to COVID-19. People in low-wage jobs tended to live in more crowded and multigenerational households where social distancing was not possible. When these people were exposed, their lack of health insurance meant they were often less willing to seek early medical treatment when symptoms arose. This led to an increased risk of serious illness from COVID-19.

As the country went into the first summer with the SARS-CoV-2 virus, the months of stress, isolation, and uncertainty began to boil over. The Black and Hispanic communities had been particularly hard-hit. Tensions were raised by a series of police killings of Black men and women. They came to a head after the death of George Floyd in Minneapolis, Minnesota.

On May 25, 2020, police arrested George Floyd for passing a counterfeit $20 bill. When he resisted arrest, they forced him to the pavement and held him down. One officer, Derek Chauvin, knelt on Floyd's neck for more than nine minutes as Floyd begged for air. Floyd died as bystanders took video of the incident, later posting these videos online for millions to see. Chauvin was eventually found guilty of second-degree murder.

Floyd's death brought the inequities in the United States to the forefront. The justice system did not treat people of different races or incomes equally. There was not much of a safety net for people in poverty

> ## ANTHONY FAUCI
>
> Anthony Fauci, the director of the National Institute of Allergy and Infectious Diseases, became the public face of the pandemic response in the early days of the COVID-19 pandemic. Fauci had led the HIV/AIDS response in the 1980s after AIDS was discovered in 1981. During the COVID-19 pandemic, he advised both President Trump and President Biden in the nation's response. He appeared in television briefings and at press conferences, explaining the emerging research about COVID-19, from prevention to treatments. Many people appreciated his ability to explain complicated scientific information in a way that was easy to understand.

when they lost their jobs, got sick, or were unfairly imprisoned. Low-wage essential workers were carrying the brunt of the burden in fighting COVID-19 while very wealthy Americans saw their fortunes soar because of the rise in the stock market or demand for certain products. As in previous pandemics, the disease brought to light inequities and provided an opportunity for reform. President Biden pushed through the American Rescue Plan, which provided help with COVID-19 relief, unemployment benefits, child tax credits, and delays on evictions. But these were all short-term solutions.

BLACK LIVES MATTER PROTESTS

Black Lives Matter, an organization that works to end discrimination and racism, held huge protests throughout the country during the summer of 2020. Most attendees wore masks. Although there were predictions that the gatherings would be super-spreader events for COVID-19, this did not occur. Researchers provided several reasons why these events did not create an uptick in cases as opening sporting events in stadiums did. Most attendees wore masks. The participants were outdoors and moving rather than sitting crowded together as in a stadium. These conditions provided good airflow and exposure to sunlight, which can destroy viruses. In addition, protesters were not sharing indoor spaces such as bathrooms and restaurants.

CHAPTER SEVEN

THE WORKFORCE CHANGES

Income inequality, the amount of separation between rich and poor people, has risen sharply in the United States in the past few decades. The middle class has not seen rising wages. People in younger generations no longer expect to do better or even as well as their parents. One reason for the divide is technology. Technology companies have far outpaced other businesses. Technology, as well as moving jobs overseas to take advantage of cheaper workers, can replace the jobs of low-income workers. For example, robots may replace assembly-line workers, and self-serve kiosks replace cashiers. Economic inequality drives social and political unrest, and the pandemic has made the differences more apparent and caused people to seek change.

The need for delivery workers increased during the pandemic because of a decrease in the number of people shopping in stores.

As with the Black Death in the 1300s and the 1918 influenza pandemic, one place societal change happened was in the labor market. As the country slowly reopened its businesses after shutdowns, employers found that they could not hire enough workers. In November 2021, job levels were still 80 percent of those before the pandemic struck.[1]

Some adults nearing 65 took early retirement rather than go back into situations that put them at risk for contracting COVID-19. Others chose to retire after they had had time to reevaluate priorities during the shutdown. Seeing friends and family lose their lives or health to COVID-19 made them realize that it might not be a good idea to postpone things they wanted to do, such as travel or spend more time with family.

> "A lot of people sacrificed a lot in the past year—the essential workers, for example—and yet they're looking at a labor market that they feel still doesn't reward them as they feel they ought to be rewarded."[2]
>
> —Joseph McCartin, executive director of the Kalmanovitz Initiative for Labor and the Working Poor at Georgetown University

Many women also left the labor market. Women were most often the primary caregivers for both children and aging parents. Many of them were still dealing with online schooling and sporadic school shutdowns and quarantines. Others decided to spend more time at home with young children. Affording childcare was another problem. Childcare centers had closed during the shutdowns. Childcare, especially for very young children, was hard to find. It was also expensive, often costing more than parents working low-paying jobs could afford.

Technology and changing attitudes of companies had increased the ease of working from remote locations. COVID-19 increased this tendency, and many companies continued to find remote working an advantage because they could hire quality workers, even those who lived

TEACHER SHORTAGE

The labor shortage was felt in education before the pandemic. But as schools reopened, there was a drastic shortage of teachers and other school staff such as aides, bus drivers, janitors, and kitchen workers. Some school districts, including those in Houston, Texas, and in South Dakota, were hundreds of teachers short. According to a survey by the National Education Association, 32 percent of teachers said the pandemic made them leave teaching earlier than they expected.[3]

far away. For those companies who preferred their workers to work on-site, they found an increased demand for childcare facilities, flexible hours, and subsidized commutes to work to draw the best workforce.

MEETING LABOR'S DEMANDS

Often, people who returned to the workforce did not stay with their previous jobs. By August 2021, experts had identified a phenomenon that became known as the Great Resignation. A record number of people quit their jobs, dissatisfied with pay or working conditions. People found that in the tight labor market, employers were not as insistent on employees' formal qualifications as long

> ### FILM WORKERS STRIKE
> The International Alliance of Theatrical Stage Employees, which represents people who work as camera operators, as makeup artists, and in other behind-the-scenes production jobs, threatened to strike in October 2021. The strike of 60,000 employees would have shut down production companies that produced content for many streaming services such as Netflix and Disney+.[4] Production had been delayed during the shutdown, and companies were demanding employees work 14-hour days to make up time. The strike was narrowly averted when companies met demands for more pay and better working conditions.

Workers at the John Deere facility in Waterloo, Iowa, went on strike in October 2021.

as they could do the job. For example, some technology companies hired apprentices to fill jobs.[5] The apprentices were trained on the job rather than getting their education in a college.

As large businesses reopened, they found that employees were not willing to go back to work on the same terms as when they had left. Workers held strikes to demand better pay, safer working conditions, and better benefits. At John Deere, which manufactures farm and construction machinery, 10,000 United Auto Workers employees walked out on October 14 and settled on November 17, winning a 10 percent raise.[6]

COVID-19 BY THE NUMBERS

BUSINESS STOCK PRICES

The stock market involves the practice of buying and selling stocks. Stocks are investments that people make in companies. The companies use these investments to try to grow. If the companies do grow and become more successful, the demand for their stocks, and therefore the prices of their stocks, go up. Investors can then sell their stocks for a profit. Different businesses had varying levels of success during the COVID-19 pandemic. Some, such as video conferencing app Zoom and online delivery service Amazon, grew throughout the pandemic. Others, such as Delta Air Lines and movie theater chain AMC Entertainment, saw declines. These successes and struggles were reflected in their stock prices.

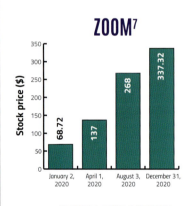

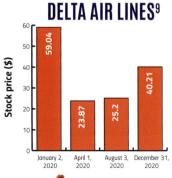

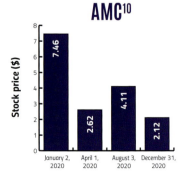

President Biden voiced support for labor, with some of his cabinet members visiting striking workers. The US Congress pushed through legislation that would provide high-paying jobs to expand and repair the country's infrastructure. The Build Back Better bill, which was Biden's plan to provide continued help to people with low wages and to families, was stalled in Congress.

This kind of widespread push by labor to demand a larger share of the booming profits of many corporations had not been seen since the end of World War II. Workers felt they had done their part to see the country through the pandemic crisis, often taking on health risks that could be avoided by higher-income people who could work remotely. In return, they felt they should benefit from their companies' success.

NEW BUSINESSES

In 2020, Americans filed paperwork to begin 4.3 million new businesses. This was a 24 percent increase over the number of applications in 2019, and even more people filed in 2021. New business start-ups had been on the decline since 1980.[11] This trend showed a major societal shift in the economy and the way people work, though

The pandemic encouraged some to take the step toward opening their own businesses.

it remained to be seen if the shift would continue beyond the pandemic. The number of people who were self-employed hit an eight-year high in July 2021.

For many, the pandemic provided the incentive to try something they had always wanted to do. Sitting at home with uncertain futures during the lockdown, there was time to try things they may have only dreamed of. That was true for the online business Songlorious, which provides custom songs for special occasions such as birthdays and weddings. Started during the shutdown by Omayya Atout and Ellen Hodges, the business was wildly successful. As Atout said, "[The pandemic] gave us a nudge where I've always wanted to do something but I was too scared because I didn't want to lose the stability of my job."[12]

New and small businesses create the majority of new jobs. These businesses can be quicker than established businesses at adapting to changing social norms such as new forms of entertainment and new ways to shop. They can allow people to use their creative skills in new ways. For society, the move toward more new business creation marks innovation and economic growth.

BACK TO BOOKSTORES

The number of new bookstores opening increased during the COVID-19 pandemic. Many independent bookstores and even some chain bookstores suffered during the shutdown when they were not allowed to open for months. But it also gave some people the opportunity to fulfill their dream of owning a bookstore as small retailers closed and the price of rent plummeted. The American Booksellers Association membership rose from 1,701 to 1,910 in 2021, and bookstore locations increased from 2,100 to 2,496.[13] Many of the newer bookstores catered to niche audiences.

CHAPTER EIGHT

THE COVID-19 GENERATION

For young adults, the COVID-19 pandemic killed dreams, expectations, and sometimes motivation. The spring of 2020 brought separation from classmates and friends. There were no sports, which was a major blow to high school juniors and seniors hoping for a last chance for a college sports scholarship. Students could not strengthen their college or job applications with clubs or other activities. Seniors missed prom, senior trips, and their last spring break. They also missed walking across a stage for graduation. Some schools had drive-by graduations, but some had nothing at all.

For students who had planned to go to college at the end of summer, those plans became uncertain. No one knew if colleges and universities would be open for in-person classes or have available dorm rooms.

In 2020, some graduating seniors created their own proms.

> "Teenagers are grieving. They've been working hard and looking forward to these events for years, and now they don't get to attend a prom or walk across the stage for their diplomas."[3]
>
> —Nilu Rahman, Johns Hopkins Children's Center

Many students did not think it was worthwhile to spend a lot of money on tuition for online classes.

For young adults going into the job market, there were few prospects. Many young adults worked at low-paying jobs in entertainment, dining, or small businesses. These jobs were not available because of shutdowns. Between January and February 2020, 2.6 million young adults moved back in with their parents at a time when they wanted to be gaining independence.[1]

Mental health was worse among young adults than older people. In October 2021, nearly 48 percent of people ages 18 to 29 reported symptoms of anxiety or depression.[2] The percentage of people experiencing these symptoms decreased with age. In the first year of the pandemic shutdowns, from March 2020 to March 2021, one poll found that 46 percent of parents reported a new or worsening mental health issue in their children.

Girls were more likely to show signs of depression and anxiety than boys. Parents of girls reported 31 percent experienced depression or sadness compared with 18 percent of boys, and 36 percent of girls felt anxiety or worry compared with 19 percent of boys.[4]

THE LOST GENERATION OF 1918

The COVID-19 pandemic, like other pandemics in the past, is expected to change life for the young generations who lived through it. Children born during the 1918 pandemic showed lifelong health effects. There were many miscarriages in mothers who caught the flu because their bodies used resources normally provided to the fetus to fight the disease. A high number of babies who were born to mothers who had the flu had both physical and cognitive problems as adults. They were more likely to have heart attacks, and possibly because of their cognitive issues, they were more likely to go to prison.

YOUNG ADULTS

For young adults, COVID-19 would change their lives forever. Their lives had already been disrupted by shifts in society after the war on terror of the early 2000s, the Great Recession of 2008, the lack of affordable housing, millions owed in student debt, and the onset of climate change. Now a pandemic had changed society again.

One way researchers gauge the stress put on a generation is through birth rate. Even before the pandemic, young people were putting off having children.

Besides greater opportunities for women in the workforce, debt, poor job opportunities, political gridlock, and pessimism about the future decreased the desire of people to have children. The birth rate in the United States had been declining for ten years and fell by an additional 4 percent in 2020.[5] Many young people were distrustful of the institutions that previous generations had built. They noted the huge disparity of income, lack of affordable health care, the slipping of US prestige in the world, and the inaction of governments in fighting climate change as proof that changes need to be made.

ACEDIA

After spending months at home adapting to video calls and keeping busy with cooking, some people didn't really feel like doing anything—everything seemed unimportant. They felt sluggish, apathetic, bored, and listless. People with these feelings may be experiencing acedia. Acedia is the feeling of melancholy. It is a feeling that what a person is doing, or has spent much of life doing, is not important when faced with struggles such as a global pandemic. It arises from months of isolation, so it was first identified in medieval monks. If the future is so uncertain, people may wonder what they are working for. The things people value change with an uncertain future. While there is little doubt that life will eventually go back to some form of normalcy, what that future will look like and how each individual will fit in is unknown.

Video calls allowed friends and family to stay in touch without visiting in person.

As lockdowns kept people separated from friends and family, many young adults turned to social media to try to maintain some sort of community. However, social media is no substitute for in-person relationships. Social media makes it easier to interact mainly with people who hold similar thoughts and beliefs. This can make it easier to form prejudices and stereotypes about people who think differently. And when someone who thinks differently is encountered, the social cues that one could normally pick up on with an in-person conversation are missed, resulting in a greater chance of heated arguments and polarization.

The long-term effects of having COVID-19 are still being studied. The initial reports emphasized the risk of contracting COVID-19 for older people, but about 20 percent of people hospitalized in early 2020 were ages 20 to 44. One in eight of those hospitalized were admitted to intensive care.[6] Since the virus is known to attack organs other than the lungs, including the heart, many young people may face lifelong health effects.

LONG COVID

Some people who had COVID-19 had symptoms that persisted for months after the infection was over, often keeping them from returning to normal life. The most common symptoms were fatigue, shortness of breath, cough, joint pain, and chest pain. Others reported difficulty thinking or concentrating as if they were in a mental fog. These long-lasting symptoms are called long COVID. Long COVID can happen to people who have mild symptoms of the disease. For young people, these persistent symptoms may keep them from moving forward with education, jobs, or starting families.

GENERATION Z

The pandemic had a different significance for Generation Z, defined as those born after 1997. They were coming of age as SARS-CoV-2 struck, the leading edge of the generation being 23 years old. The people of Generation Z grew up in a world where schools had frequent lockdown drills to prepare for potential shootings. The oldest of them were only two years old when the mass shooting at Columbine High School shocked the nation and brought lockdown drills into schools. For Gen Z, terrorism has always been a topic in the news—the oldest members were only starting kindergarten when terrorists attacked the United States on September 11, 2001. They were still in elementary school when the Great Recession of 2008 cost thousands of people their jobs and homes.

When COVID-19 hit, many were in the formative years of high school and college. For young adults whose personalities were forming and changing, it was a time when many began to question the future. Among high school students, 44 percent reported they would likely change their education plans because of COVID-19. When thinking about college, 40 percent were reconsidering whether getting a higher education was worth the cost and effort. Employed members of Gen Z questioned whether getting an education or building a business or career was worth the effort. Because of the pandemic, 43 percent of Gen Z changed their career focus, and 48 percent considered changing their careers.[7]

COPING WITH COVID-19

Dr. Lisa Damour, an adolescent psychologist and best-selling author, suggested six ways that teens could help themselves cope with the pandemic. First, they needed to realize that they were not the only ones feeling anxiety about school closings and illness. They needed to do what they could to protect themselves, such as washing hands and getting reliable sources for information. Second, they could distract themselves with movies, books, or hobbies. Third, it was important to connect with others through social media but not get drawn into too much screen time. Fourth, they could do something they have always wanted to try, such as learn to play an instrument. Fifth, they could move forward by recognizing their feelings of sadness or disappointment, and then doing something that made them feel positive. And finally, they needed to be kind and thoughtful about what others were going through.

Cultures and societal norms are eventually defined by younger generations as they gain financial power and raise their own children. People might get a peek of what the future will look like by examining the values of the generation most affected by the coronavirus. Richard Flory, who studies religious and cultural change, stated, "This [COVID-19] crisis will be one of the formative experiences of most young people's lives. They are watching how their parents, cities, schools and government act. It's [making obvious] the inability of large-scale institutions to address these issues."[8] Flory said

Safety precautions were put in place for graduations during the pandemic.

that young people already have a mistrust of institutions but that because US culture tends to lean heavily toward individualism, people will continue to have trouble working together with large groups to enact change.

CHAPTER NINE

HOW HAVE WE CHANGED?

By the end of 2020, one out of every 1,000 people in the United States had died of COVID-19. That was the official number, but one study showed that up to 35 percent of deaths due to the disease were reported incorrectly as being from a different cause. Total deaths in the United States rose by 17 percent for the year. According to the CDC, that made 2020 the deadliest year in US history.[1] The United States had almost 2.5 times the death rate of Canada. With only 4 percent of the world's population, the United States had accounted for 20 percent of COVID-19 deaths by February 2021.[2]

Each person experienced the pandemic differently. Those in poverty and people of color disproportionately lost loved ones and were financially devastated. Other people were isolated from the worst of the disease.

COVID-19 changed the structure of people's lives. Certain services, such as delivery services, became much more widely used.

Some people were returning to life as normal by 2021. Others would have long-term physical and mental health issues as well as financial ones. The crisis brought out behaviors that at times showed selfishness or a lack of empathy. It emphasized divides between rich and poor and between young and old.

The lockdowns may have changed some people's personalities. Although personality is fairly stable once people become adults, research shows that extreme events, such as being isolated from others, may cause changes. Time for self-reflection or extreme stress may have positive or negative effects on how people feel and behave. It is too early to tell if changes are permanent, but people may find that even those close to them have had some personality changes.

Many people on the front lines of the fight against COVID-19 were traumatized by their experiences. Nurses had to refuse to let family in to see dying patients. They had to reuse personal protective equipment, putting themselves and their patients at risk. Doctors had to make decisions about who got treatment when supplies ran short. People struggled with having to isolate themselves from parents and grandparents. Trauma can last a long time after the cause of the trauma is gone.

FULL SPEED AHEAD

Cultural change is often accelerated by a crisis. The COVID-19 pandemic accelerated many changes that were already happening. In employment, more companies moved to automate jobs, replacing people with machines that could do work faster and cheaper. Retail jobs, such as cashiers and stockers, were reduced as more people shopped online. A survey by McKinsey and Company found that 30 to 49 percent of people expected to buy more groceries online in the future.[3]

WILL ROBOTS TAKE YOUR JOB?

Automation has moved faster into the workforce with the shortage of workers due to COVID-19. Although automation creates jobs in software design and repair of systems, it decreases the number of low-paying jobs, especially in the service industry. Robots are taking over jobs once done by people, such as tossing pizza dough, delivering room service in hotels, and cleaning floors. Some restaurants are moving to smartphone apps that let the customer order and pay from the table without a server or cashier. Artificial intelligence may even replace the jobs of fitness trainers and financial advisers.

Certain forms of health care were also moving online. Many doctors began using telemedicine instead of in-person appointments. People adapted to this new way of getting health care due to a fear of going out, especially to hospitals or doctors' offices. Anxiety and depression had more than tripled between 2019 and 2020. Mental health therapy surged with online options.

Although full-time online education has not worked well for most public school students, teachers are likely to use online lessons more in their classrooms. Students may eventually opt to take some classes entirely online.

Travel has also changed. People became accustomed to stricter security at airports after terrorists hijacked airplanes on September 11, 2001, and crashed them into key buildings in New York City and Virginia. In the same way, people are now accustomed to stricter health checks when they travel. Airplanes, hotels, and other venues spend more time and money on sanitizing and will adopt no-touch options such as key cards or automated bathroom fixtures such as faucets and soap dispensers that turn on when they sense a person's hands moving.

The biggest change will likely be reliance on technology. When the country shut down, people depended on technology for shopping, education, entertainment, banking, and communication. Although many people had already come to depend on technology, the pandemic brought technology to the forefront as a necessity.

> ## NEW LANGUAGE
> People invented new terms or resurrected old ones to deal with the new reality of the COVID-19 world. People began talking about Zoom meetings and Zoom bombing, or popping in on someone else's Zoom meetings. *Social distancing* was added to the Oxford English Dictionary in 2020, defined as the prescribed distance required to provide protection from the spread of SARS-CoV-2. People also became familiar with medical terms that were adopted into social conversation, such as PPE, which stands for personal protective equipment, and N95, which was one of the most effective face masks for blocking viruses.

PROS AND CONS

In a study by Pew Research in August 2020, 89 percent of people mentioned the pandemic had negative impacts on their lives. However, there were some silver linings. Seventy-three percent found at least one good thing that had resulted from the pandemic.[4]

In personal relationships, people found both negative and positive impacts. Negative impacts included missing family and friends, as well as losing touch with colleagues and other people in their lives. Some felt isolated, while others felt living in crowded conditions was a

PANDEMIC OR ENDEMIC

Toward the end of 2021, people began talking about COVID-19 moving from being a pandemic to an endemic disease. Becoming endemic meant that the number of infections would stabilize instead of having the peaks and valleys of infection rates that caused disruption in society. With Omicron infecting so many people, that did not happen. Still, Omicron could provide enough people with some immunity to avoid overwhelming the system. When health-care workers, governments, and the public consider the disease no longer a crisis but view it more like the seasonal flu, COVID-19 will be considered endemic.

negative impact. On the positive side, people had more time to spend with others in their household. Some also created more time for geographically distant friends and relatives by having video chats. People younger than 50 were more likely to find positive changes in relationships than those older than 50.[5]

In the amount and quality of free time people experienced, 32 percent thought the pandemic had a negative impact while 26 percent thought it had a positive impact. Almost half of people over 65 found more disruption in how they spent their free time when they were unable to travel or go out. Only about one-quarter of people under 50 had a similar experience. About one-quarter of people appreciated having more time for hobbies, to do things around the house, or just to relax more than they had in the past.[6]

In terms of physical and mental health, 28 percent thought the pandemic had negative impacts. Many people experienced death or illness in their families. They had more stress due to jobs or financial issues. Lack of exercise caused poorer health. One in three women faced health issues compared with one in five men. However, 14 percent of people found some positive health results.[7]

Some people chose to make lifestyle changes, such as exercising more frequently, during the pandemic.

Some mentioned having more time for healthy eating and exercise, appreciating important things in life, and also having less stressful schedules.

In their own jobs and the jobs of people they knew, 23 percent found negative effects while 13 found positive effects. Positive effects, such as working from home leading to more productivity and less commute time, were most often reported by people with college educations and higher incomes. People with a high school diploma or less were twice as likely to lose their jobs or have reduced hours.[8] Essential workers, such as teachers and health-care workers, had much more stress as students moved online and hospitals filled with patients.

New York City celebrated essential workers in a 2021 Hometown Heroes parade.

When it came to personal finances and the nation's economy generally, 22 percent of Americans felt the pandemic had a negative effect, while 13 percent found some positive effect. One in three Americans had used part of their savings to pay expenses, and one in four had a problem paying bills.[9] Those who reported a positive impact on finances reported that they had saved money by not spending on recreation or dining out.

Most people had never dealt with a major pandemic. The last one was more than 100 years ago. Reactions to shifting social norms and the changes brought by lockdowns were different for different people. But one thing was the same for everyone. As was true for past pandemics, people will live in a new postpandemic world, and some things will never be the same again.

> "After the Black Death, nothing was the same. What I expect now is something as dramatic is going to happen, not so much in medicine but in economy and culture. Because of danger, there's this wonderful human response, which is to think in a new way."[10]
>
> —Gianna Pomata, professor emerita at Johns Hopkins University

ESSENTIAL FACTS

KEY EVENTS

- On March 5, 2020, the first school district closes in Washington, beginning more than a year of school closures across the country.

- On March 22, 2020, a statewide shutdown of New York begins.

- From March 2020 to March 2021, 46 percent of parents report a new or worsening mental health issue in their children.

- On April 3, 2021, the first theater on Broadway reopens after a year of shutdown.

- By November 1, 2021, the United States has 70 percent of adults fully vaccinated, but hope for an end to the disease is thwarted by the Omicron variant.

KEY PEOPLE

- Anthony Fauci, director of the National Institute of Allergy and Infectious Diseases, was the public face of the health science community during the pandemic.

- Donald Trump was the US president when COVID-19 hit in early 2020. At first he rejected masks, but later he began wearing them. He supported the efforts to quickly produce a vaccine.

- President Joe Biden took office in January 2021 and continued the effort to get people vaccinated and to pass the Build Back Better bill, which would provide relief for low-wage workers, especially parents.

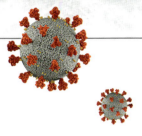

- Low-income workers are a high percentage of essential workers, who had to risk exposure to COVID-19 to keep their jobs. Many began demanding better wages and benefits as compensation for the essential work they do, pushing some companies to meet these demands and changing the landscape of industries.

KEY STATISTICS

- American Indians died at twice the rate of white people, increasing awareness about inequity between people of different races.
- In the first months of the pandemic, cases of depression in adults rose from 8.5 to 27.8 percent.
- Testing at the end of the 2020–2021 school year showed students on average were 3 to 6 percent behind in reading and 8 to 12 percent behind in math compared with the previous year.
- Approximately half of Gen Z changed their education or career plans because of COVID-19.

QUOTE

"This [COVID-19] crisis will be one of the formative experiences of most young people's lives. They are watching how their parents, cities, schools and government act. It's [making obvious] the inability of large-scale institutions to address these issues."

—Richard Flory, who studies religious and cultural change

GLOSSARY

epidemic
The rapid spreading of a disease so that many people have it at the same time.

genetics
The combination of traits that parents pass on to their children.

hybrid
Something that is part one thing and part something else.

immune system
A bodily system that protects the body from foreign particles such as bacteria and viruses.

immunity
Resistance to disease.

impeached
Charged with misconduct while in office.

incentive
A reason to do something or change an action.

innovative
Having to do with new ideas or actions.

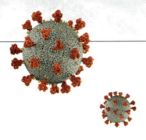

lockdown
Time during COVID-19 when most businesses, schools, and more were closed and most travel was restricted to help control the spread of the virus.

pharmaceutical
Having to do with medications and their production and sale.

quarantine
To physically isolate, particularly for people who are ill and possibly contagious.

rehabilitation
The use of therapy to return someone to an improved physical or psychological function.

social distancing
Keeping a safe distance from other people to avoid catching a disease.

super-spreader
A person or event that infects a large number of other people.

variant
A strain of a virus that may contain one or more mutations.

ADDITIONAL RESOURCES

SELECTED BIBLIOGRAPHY

Christakis, Nicholas A. *Apollo's Arrow: The Profound and Enduring Impact of Coronavirus on the Way We Live*. Little, Brown Spark, 2020.

Gottlieb, Scott. *Uncontrolled Spread: Why COVID-19 Crushed Us and How We Can Defeat the Next Pandemic*. Harper, 2021.

Wright, Lawrence. *The Plague Year: America in the Time of COVID*. Alfred P. Knopf, 2021.

FURTHER READINGS

Gale, Ryan. *Joe Biden: 46th US President*. Abdo, 2021.

Gresko, Marcia S. *COVID-19 and the Challenges of the New Normal*. ReferencePoint, 2021.

Idzikowski, Lisa, ed. *The Politics and Science of COVID-19*. Greenhaven, 2022.

ONLINE RESOURCES

To learn more about society and culture during COVID-19, please visit **abdobooklinks.com** or scan this QR code. These links are routinely monitored and updated to provide the most current information available.

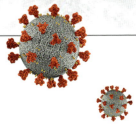

MORE INFORMATION

For more information on this subject, contact or visit the following organizations:

NATIONAL EDUCATION ASSOCIATION

1201 16th St. NW
Washington, DC 20036
202-833-4000
nea.org

The National Education Association is an organization that promotes equality in the education system. Its research on student access to technology helped people understand the disadvantages of distance learning early on in the pandemic.

NATIONAL INSTITUTE OF MENTAL HEALTH (NIMH)

6001 Executive Blvd., Room 6200, MSC 9663
Bethesda, MD 20892
1-866-615-6464
nimh.nih.gov

The National Institute of Mental Health (NIMH) is the government's lead organization on research into mental health. It has ongoing research into how to reduce mental health disparities based on age, gender, ethnicity, and other factors.

SOURCE NOTES

CHAPTER 1. THE SHUTDOWN
1. Jesse McKinley. "New York City Region Is Now an Epicenter of the Coronavirus Pandemic." *New York Times*, 22 Mar. 2020, nytimes.com. Accessed 14 Mar. 2022.
2. Lawrence Wright. *The Plague Year: America in the Time of COVID*. Knopf, 2021. 158.
3. Laura Santhanam. "COVID Helped Cause the Biggest Drop in US Life Expectancy Since WWII." *PBS*, 22 Dec. 2021, pbs.org. Accessed 14 Mar. 2022.
4. Jenny Howard. "Plague Was One of History's Deadliest Diseases—Then We Found a Cure." *National Geographic*, 6 July 2020, nationalgeographic.com. Accessed 16 Mar. 2022.
5. "1918 Pandemic (H1N1 Virus)." *CDC*, 20 Mar. 2019, cdc.gov. Accessed 14 Mar. 2022.
6. "1918 Pandemic (H1N1 Virus)."
7. Amanda Barroso. "About Half of Americans Say Their Lives Will Remain Changed in Major Ways When the Pandemic Is Over." *Pew Research Center*, 17 Sept. 2020, pewresearch.org. Accessed 14 Mar. 2022.
8. Cara Murez. "COVID Has Killed More Americans Than the Spanish Flu Did in 1918." *US News*, 21 Sept. 2021, usnews.com. Accessed 14 Mar. 2022.
9. "How Pandemics Shape Society." *Johns Hopkins University*, 9 Apr. 2020, hub.jhu.edu. Accessed 14 Mar. 2022.

CHAPTER 2. FIRST CASUALTIES: THE ELDERLY
1. Eric Boodman and Helen Branswell. "First COVID-19 Outbreak in a US Nursing Home Raises Concerns." *STAT*, 29 Feb. 2020, statnews.com. Accessed 14 Mar. 2022.
2. Boodman and Branswell, "First COVID-19 Outbreak in a US Nursing Home Raises Concerns."
3. Michael Gold and Ed Shanahan. "What We Know About Cuomo's Nursing Home Scandal." *New York Times*, 4 Aug. 2021, nytimes.com. Accessed 14 Mar. 2022.
4. "COVID-19 in Nursing Homes: Most Homes Had Multiple Outbreaks and Weeks of Sustained Transmission from May 2020 through January 2021." *GAO*, 19 May 2021, gao.gov. Accessed 14 Mar. 2022.
5. "COVID-19 in Nursing Homes."
6. Priya Chidambaram and Rachel Garfield. "Nursing Homes Experienced Steeper Increase In COVID-19 Cases and Deaths in August 2021 Than the Rest of the Country." *KFF*, 1 Oct. 2021, kff.org. Accessed 14 Mar. 2022.
7. Beth Schwartzapfel, Katie Park, and Andrew Demillo. "1 in 5 Prisoners in the US Has Had COVID-19." *Marshall Project*, 18 Dec. 2020, themarshallproject.org. Accessed 14 Mar. 2022.
8. Lawrence Wright. *The Plague Year: America in the Time of COVID*. Knopf, 2021. 160.
9. Wright, *The Plague Year*. 160.
10. Louise Aronson. "For Older People, Despair, as Well as Covid-19, Is Costing Lives." *New York Times*, 8 June 2020, nytimes.com. Accessed 14 Mar. 2022.
11. Reginald D. Williams II, Arnav Shah, Michelle M. Doty, Katharine Fields, and Molly FitzGerald. "The Impact of COVID-19 on Older Adults." *Commonwealth Fund*, 15 Sept. 2021, commonwealthfund.org. Accessed 14 Mar. 2022.
12. Federica Cocco. "Millennials Grow More Resentful Towards Older Generations as Restrictions, Economic Fallout Hit Them Harder." *Financial Post*, 17 Nov. 2020, financialpost.com. Accessed 14 Mar. 2022.
13. Jack Healy. "Tribal Elders Are Dying from the Pandemic, Causing a Cultural Crisis for American Indians." *New York Times*, 12 Jan. 2021, nytimes.com. Accessed 14 Mar. 2022.
14. Healy, "Tribal Elders Are Dying from the Pandemic."

CHAPTER 3. NO MORE SCHOOL
1. Lauren Camera. "Lessons Learned from a Year of Closed Schools." *US News*, 9 Mar. 2021, usnews.com. Accessed 22 Mar. 2022.
2. "The Digital Divide and Homework Gap in Your State." *NEA*, 16 Oct. 2020, nea.org. Accessed 14 Mar. 2022.
3. David Robson. "How COVID-19 is Changing the World's Children." *BBC*, 3 June 2020, bbc.com. Accessed 14 Mar. 2022.

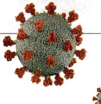

    4. Matt Barnum. "The Pandemic's Toll: National Test Scores Show Progress Slowed, Gaps Widened." *Chalkbeat*, 28 July 2021, chalkbeat.org. Accessed 14 Mar. 2022.
    5. Camera, "Lessons Learned from a Year of Closed Schools."
    6. Camera, "Lessons Learned from a Year of Closed Schools."
    7. Camera, "Lessons Learned from a Year of Closed Schools."
    8. "National School Lunch Program." *USDA*, 13 Jan. 2022, ers.usda.gov. Accessed 14 Mar. 2022.
    9. Robson, "How COVID-19 Is Changing the World's Children."
    10. Robson, "How COVID-19 Is Changing the World's Children."

CHAPTER 4. WORKING FROM HOME

    1. Lawrence Wright. *The Plague Year: America in the Time of COVID*. Knopf, 2021. 158.
    2. Kim Parker, Juliana Menasce Horowitz, and Rachel Minkin. "How the Coronavirus Outbreak Has—and Hasn't—Changed the Way Americans Work." *Pew Research Center*, 9 Dec. 2020, pewresearch.org. Accessed 15 Mar. 2022.
    3. Parker et al., "How the Coronavirus Outbreak Has—and Hasn't—Changed the Way Americans Work."
    4. Kelli Kennedy. "COVID-19 Pet Boom Has Veterinarians Backlogged, Burned Out." *AP News*, 12 May 2021, apnews.com. Accessed 15 Mar. 2022.
    5. "The Pandemic Pet Boom." *Week*, 15 Aug. 2021, theweek.com. Accessed 15 Mar. 2022.
    6. Kennedy, "COVID-19 Pet Boom Has Veterinarians Backlogged."
    7. Parker et al., "How the Coronavirus Outbreak Has—and Hasn't—Changed the Way Americans Work."
    8. Parker et al., "How the Coronavirus Outbreak Has—and Hasn't—Changed the Way Americans Work."
    9. Parker et al., "How the Coronavirus Outbreak Has—and Hasn't—Changed the Way Americans Work."
    10. Avery Van Etten. "Survey Finds Majority of Parents Want to Continue Remote Work Post-Pandemic." *ABC News*, 23 June 2021, abc27.com. Accessed 15 Mar. 2022.
    11. Kelsey Snell. "What's Inside The Senate's $2 Trillion Coronavirus Aid Package." *NPR*, 26 Mar. 2020, npr.org. Accessed 15 Mar. 2022.
    12. Elizabeth Rosner. "US Divorce Rates Skyrocket amid COVID-19 Pandemic." *New York Post*, 1 Sept. 2020, nypost.com. Accessed 15 Mar. 2022.
    13. Usha Ranji, Brittni Frederiksen, Alina Salganicoff, and Michelle Long. "Women, Work, and Family During COVID-19: Findings from the KFF Women's Health Survey." *KFF*, 22 Mar. 2021, kff.org. Accessed 15 Mar. 2022.
    14. Tonya Mosley and Serena McMahon. "How To Mitigate Loneliness And Its Consequences." *WBUR*, 20 Aug. 2022, wbur.org. Accessed 15 Mar. 2022.
    15. Ranji et al., "Women, Work, and Family During COVID-19: Findings from the KFF Women's Health Survey."
    16. Ranji et al., "Women, Work, and Family During COVID-19: Findings from the KFF Women's Health Survey."
    17. Jillian McKoy. "Depression Rates in US Tripled When the Pandemic First Hit—Now, They're Even Worse." *Brink*, 7 Oct. 2021, bu.edu. Accessed 15 Mar. 2022.
    18. McKoy, "Depression Rates in US Tripled When the Pandemic First Hit."
    19. Carol P. Motley, MD, and Charlotte C. Linder, MD. "Together—The Healing Power of Human Connection in a Sometimes Lonely World." *Family Medicine*, 2021, journals.stfm.org. Accessed 15 Mar. 2022.

CHAPTER 5. ENTERTAINMENT

    1. Joumana Khatib. "How the Pandemic Changed the Way We Read." *New York Times*, 10 Mar. 2021, nytimes.com. Accessed 15 Mar. 2022.
    2. Rebecca Bodenheimer. "What's Behind the Pandemic Puzzle Craze?" *JSTOR Daily*, 16 Dec. 2020, daily.jstor.org. Accessed 15 Mar. 2022.

SOURCE NOTES CONTINUED

3. Drew Weisholtz. "How Classic Board Games are Bringing Families Closer During the Pandemic." *Today*, 5 Dec. 2020, today.com. Accessed 15 Mar. 2022.

4. Ryan Faughnder. "What Zoom Fatigue? Pandemic Virtual Concerts May Have Changed Live Music Forever." *Los Angeles Times*, 24 June 2021, latimes.com. Accessed 15 Mar. 2022.

5. Michael Paulson. "Broadway, Symbol of New York Resilience, Shuts Down Amid Virus Threat." *New York Times*, 12 May 2020, nytimes.com. Accessed 15 Mar. 2022.

6. Bill Carter. "We Can't Stop Watching TV During the Pandemic—And That's OK." *CNN*, 10 Apr. 2020, cnn.com. Accessed 15 Mar. 2022.

7. David Lange. "COVID-19: Impact of Fan Attendance on Sports Enjoyment on TV 2020." *Statista*, 21 Sept. 2021, statista.com. Accessed 15 Mar. 2022.

CHAPTER 6. POLITICS AND DIVISION

1. Patrick van Kessel, Chris Baronavski, Alissa Scheller, and Aaron Smith. "In Their Own Words, Americans Describe the Struggles and Silver Linings of the COVID-19 Pandemic." *Pew Research Center*, 5 Mar. 2021, pewresearch.org. Accessed 15 Mar. 2022.

2. "Coronavirus: Donald Trump Wears Face Mask for the First Time." *BBC*, 12 July 2020, bbc.com. Accessed 15 Mar. 2022.

3. Lynne Peeples. "Face Masks: What the Data Say." *Nature*, 6 Oct. 2020, nature.com. Accessed 15 Mar. 2022.

4. Peeples, "Face Masks."

5. Audrey Carlsen, Pien Huang, Zach Levitt, and Daniel Wood. "How Are the COVID-19 Vaccine and Booster Campaigns Going in Your State?" *NPR*, 14 Mar. 2022, npr.org. Accessed 15 Mar. 2022.

6. Alexander Tin. "U.S. Falls Short of Biden's July 4 COVID-19 Vaccine Goal." *CBS News*, 4 July 2021, cbsnews.com. Accessed 15 Mar. 2022.

7. Tin, "U.S. Falls Short of Biden's July 4 COVID-19 Vaccine Goal."

8. Kevin Breuninger and Spencer Kimball. "Supreme Court Blocks Biden Covid Vaccine Mandate for Businesses, Allows Health-Care Worker Rule." *CNBC*, 13 Jan. 2022, cnbc.com. Accessed 15 Mar. 2022.

9. Mychael Schnell. "70% of US Adults Are Fully Vaccinated, 80% Partially: White House." *Hill*, 1 Nov. 2021, thehill.com. Accessed 15 Mar. 2022.

10. David Leonhardt. "Omicron Threatens Red America." *New York Times*, 17 Dec. 2021, nytimes.com. Accessed 15 Mar. 2022.

11. Lawrence Wright. *The Plague Year: America in the Time of COVID*. Knopf, 2021. 242.

12. "Remarks by President Biden Before Meeting on COVID-19." *White House*, 4 Jan. 2022, whitehouse.gov. Accessed 16 Mar. 2022.

13. Justin Lo, Krutika Amin Twitter, Dustin Cotliar, Matthew Rae Twitter, and Cynthia Cox. "COVID-19 Breakthrough Hospitalizations." *Health System Tracker*, 15 Dec. 2021, healthsystemtracker.org. Accessed 15 Mar. 2022.

14. Edouard Mathieu and Max Roser. "How Do Death Rates From COVID-19 Differ Between People Who Are Vaccinated and Those Who Are Not?" *Our World in Data*, 23 Nov. 2021, ourworldindata.org. Accessed 15 Mar. 2022.

15. Zach Levitt and Dan Keating. "Mapping America's Hospitalization and Vaccination Divide." *Washington Post*, 23 Sept. 2021, washingtonpost.com. Accessed 15 Mar. 2022.

16. Mitch Smith, Julie Bosman and Tracey Tully. "Omicron Cases Appear to Peak in US, but Deaths Continue to Rise." *New York Times*, 22 Jan. 2022, nytimes.com. Accessed 16 Mar. 2022.

17. "US COVID-19 Vaccine Tracker: See Your State's Progress." *Mayo Clinic*, 2022, mayoclinic.org. Accessed 15 Mar. 2022.

CHAPTER 7. THE WORKFORCE CHANGES

1. Alejandra Marquez Janse, Ailsa Chang, Courtney Dorning, and Matt Ozug. "Three Reasons Labor Strikes Are Surging Right Now — And Why They Could Continue To Grow." *NPR*, 2 Nov. 2021, npr.org. Accessed 15 Mar. 2022.

2. Marquez Janse et al., "Three Reasons Labor Strikes Are Surging Right Now."

3. Jocelyn Gecker. "COVID-19 Creates Dire US Shortage of Teachers, School Staff." *AP News*, 22 Sept. 2021, apnews.com. Accessed 15 Mar. 2022.

4. Lisa Richwine and Bhargav Acharya. "Hollywood Film-Crew Union Reaches Tentative Deal, Averting Strike." *Reuters*, 18 Oct. 2021, reuters.com. Accessed 15 Mar. 2022.

5. Jeanne Sahadi. "No College Degree? More Employers Than Ever Just Don't Care." *CNN*, 12 Oct. 2021, cnn.com. Accessed 15 Mar. 2022.

6. "John Deere Strike Ends after Workers OK Pact with Hefty Raises in Third Vote." *CBS News*, 18 Nov. 2021, cbsnews.com. Accessed 15 Mar. 2022.

7. "Zoom Video Communications, Inc. (ZM)." *Yahoo Finance*, 2022, finance.yahoo.com. Accessed 15 Mar. 2022.

8. "Amazon.com, Inc. (AMZN)." *Yahoo Finance*, 2022, finance.yahoo.com. Accessed 15 Mar. 2022.

9. "Delta Air Lines, Inc. (DAL)." *Yahoo Finance*, 2022, finance.yahoo.com. Accessed 15 Mar. 2022.

10. "AMC Entertainment Holdings, Inc. (AMC)." *Yahoo Finance*, 2022, finance.yahoo.com. Accessed 15 Mar. 2022.

11. Ben Casselman. "Start-Up Boom in the Pandemic Is Growing Stronger." *New York Times*, 19 Aug. 2021, nytimes.com. Accessed 15 Mar. 2022.

12. Casselman, "Start-Up Boom in the Pandemic Is Growing Stronger."

13. Judith Rosen. "Another Pandemic Surprise: A Mini Indie Bookstore Boom." *Publishers Weekly*, 15 Oct. 2021, publishersweekly.com. Accessed 15 Mar. 2022.

CHAPTER 8. THE COVID-19 GENERATION

1. Richard Fry, Jeffrey S. Passel, and D'Vera Cohn. "A Majority of Young Adults in the US Live with Their Parents for the First Time Since the Great Depression." *Pew Research Center*, 4 Sept. 2020, pewresearch.org. Accessed 16 Mar. 2022.

2. "Anxiety and Depression." *CDC*, 16 Feb. 2022, cdc.gov. Accessed 15 Mar. 2022.

3. Nilu Rahman, MS, CCLS. "Staying at Home During COVID-19: How to Help Teens Cope." *Johns Hopkins Medicine*, 16 June 2020, hopkinsmedicine.org. Accessed 15 Mar. 2022.

4. Beata Mostafavi. "National Poll: Pandemic Negatively Impacted Teens' Mental Health." *Michigan Health*, 15 Mar. 2021, healthblog.uofmhealth.org. Accessed 15 Mar. 2022.

5. "Baby Bust: Explaining the Declining U.S. Birth Rate." *NPR*, 26 July 2021, npr.org. Accessed 15 Mar. 2022.

6. Gary Polakovic. "How Does Coronavirus Affect Young People's Psyches?" *USC News*, 25 Mar. 2020, news.usc.edu. Accessed 15 Mar. 2022.

7. "The State of Gen Z 2020." *Center for Generational Kinetics*, 2020, msjc.edu. Accessed 15 Mar. 2022.

8. Polakovic, "How Does Coronavirus Affect Young People's Psyches?"

CHAPTER 9. HOW HAVE WE CHANGED?

1. Lawrence Wright. *The Plague Year: America in the Time of COVID*. Knopf, 2021. 241.

2. Wright, *The Plague Year*. 241.

3. Vinayak Kumar and Ram Prasad Modalavalasa. "Five Lasting Changes from the COVID-19 Pandemic." *ABC News*, 16 Aug. 2020, abcnews.go.com. Accessed 15 Mar. 2022.

4. Patrick van Kessel, Chris Baronavski, Alissa Scheller, and Aaron Smith. "In Their Own Words, Americans Describe the Struggles and Silver Linings of the COVID-19 Pandemic." *Pew Research Center*, 5 Mar. 2021, pewresearch.org. Accessed 15 Mar. 2022.

5. van Kessel et al., "In Their Own Words."

6. van Kessel et al., "In Their Own Words."

7. van Kessel et al., "In Their Own Words."

8. van Kessel et al., "In Their Own Words."

9. van Kessel et al., "In Their Own Words."

10. Wright, *The Plague Year*. 108.

INDEX

abuse, 34–35
Amazon, 76
AMC Entertainment, 76
American Indians, 23–25
American Rescue Plan, 69
automation, 93–94

bats, 9
Biden, Joe, 63–64, 66, 68, 69, 77
birth rate, 83–84
Black Death, the, 9, 58, 72
Black Lives Matter, 69
board games, 48, 49
books, 45, 47, 79, 88
Broadway, 51
Build Back Better, 77

Centers for Disease Control and Prevention, US (CDC), 7, 9, 60, 91
childcare, 8, 27, 41, 44, 73–74
China, 6, 10, 15
college, 34, 75, 81, 87, 98
concerts, 49
Congress, US, 77
Coronavirus Aid, Relief, and Economic Security (CARES) Act, 41

culture, 9, 13, 23, 88–89, 93, 99
Cuomo, Andrew, 5, 16

deaths, 8, 15–20, 27, 66, 91, 97
debt, 83–84
Delta Air Lines, 76
Delta variant, 66
Democrats, 57–58, 61, 65
Denmark, 65
Department of Health and Human Services, 10
Diamond Princess, 15
disabilities, 10, 32, 43
Disney+, 48, 74
divorce, 41–42
doctors, 7, 8, 58–59, 62, 92, 94

elderly, 17–18, 20–24, 43
entertainment, 47–55, 67, 76, 79, 82, 95
essential workers, 5–6, 60, 67, 69, 72, 98
exercise, 97–98

Fauci, Anthony, 68
financial stress, 37, 65
Floyd, George, 68
free time, 96

Generation Z, 86–87
Great Recession, the, 83, 87
Great Resignation, the, 74
groceries, 5–6, 67, 93
hospitalization, 6–7, 16, 18, 20, 66, 86, 98

immunity, 18, 63, 96
inequality, 65, 68–69, 71
internet access, 29, 38, 45, 60

lockdowns, 22–23, 37, 42, 57, 78, 85, 87, 92, 99
loneliness, 45
long COVID, 86
low-income workers, 39, 43–44, 71

mask mandates, 30, 59–62
Mello, Michelle, 65
mental health, 28, 34, 45, 58, 82–83, 92, 94, 97
  acedia, 84
  anxiety, 8, 45, 47, 82–83, 88, 94
  depression, 45, 82–83, 94
movies, 28, 37, 49, 51–52, 76, 88

110

multisystem inflammatory syndrome, 28
Murthy, Vivek, 43, 45

National Education Association, 29, 73
National School Lunch Program, 33
Netflix, 48, 74
new businesses, 77–79
New York City, 5–6, 51, 65, 94
1918 influenza pandemic, 10–13, 17–18, 58, 72, 83
N95 masks, 59–60, 95
nurses, 19, 92
nursing homes, 15–17, 20, 27, 64

Olympics, 55
Omicron variant, 66, 96

parents, 18, 27–29, 33, 40, 44, 71, 73, 82–83, 88, 93
Peacock, 55
people of color, 31–32, 39, 43–44, 67–68, 91
pets, 38
Pew Research, 57, 95
Poe, Edgar Allan, 48

Policy that Assures Uniform Safety for Everyone (PAUSE) Program, 5
prisons, 16, 17, 83
protests, 65, 69

quarantines, 10, 16, 18, 49, 73

relationships, 41–42, 85, 95–96
Republicans, 57–58, 61–62, 65, 66
retail, 8, 67, 79, 93

school, 5, 13, 27–35, 37, 41, 44, 53, 57, 65, 73, 75, 81, 86, 87–88, 94–95, 98
special education, 33
screen time, 48–52, 88
severe acute respiratory syndrome coronavirus 2 (SARS-CoV-2), 6–7, 60, 67, 86, 95
social distancing, 16, 22–23, 28, 30, 41, 62, 67, 95
social media, 49–50, 85, 88
Songlorious, 78
sports, 28, 47, 53–55, 69, 81
stocks, 69, 76

strike, 74, 75
Supreme Court, US, 64
symptoms, 15–16, 28, 66, 67, 82, 86

teachers, 27, 30, 34–35, 73, 94, 98
technology, 71, 73, 75, 94–95
TikTok, 50
travel, 8, 15, 49, 67, 72, 94, 96
Trump, Donald, 57, 61–63, 68

unemployment, 37, 67, 69
United Talent Agency, 49

vaccines, 7, 12, 35, 62–65, 66

war on terror, 83, 87, 94
Warner Bros., 51
Williams, Anne, 47
women, 24, 41, 43–44, 68, 73, 84, 97
working at home, 37–41
World War II, 55, 77

Zoom, 28, 30, 50, 76, 95

111

ABOUT THE AUTHOR

CYNTHIA KENNEDY HENZEL

Cynthia Kennedy Henzel has a BS in social studies education and an MS in geography. She has worked as a teacher-educator in many countries. Currently, she writes fiction and nonfiction books and develops education materials for social studies, history, science, and English Language Learner students. She has written more than 100 books and more than 150 stories for young people.

ABOUT THE CONSULTANT

ALLEN FURR

Allen Furr is a professor emeritus of sociology at Auburn University. He received his PhD from Louisiana State University and is a former Fulbright Scholar. His main research areas are the sociology of health and medicine, and his work has been published in medical and nursing journals as well as scholarly publications in sociology.